WHAT'S OUT THE

A Book About Space

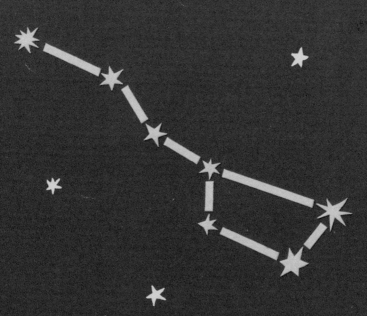

Grosset & Dunlap

Special thanks to Clint Hatchett, Technical Director and Astronomer,
Christa McAuliffe Planetarium, Concord, New Hampshire

Text copyright © 1993, 2007 by Lynn Wilson. Illustrations copyright
© 1993 by Paige Billin-Frye. All rights reserved. Published by
Grosset & Dunlap, a division of Penguin Young Readers Group,
345 Hudson Street, New York, New York 10014. GROSSET &
DUNLAP and READING RAILROAD are trademarks of Penguin
Group (USA) Inc. Printed in the U.S.A.

Library of Congress Cataloging-in-Publication Data
Wilson, Lynn, 1946- What's out there? : a book about space /
Lynn Wilson ; illustrated by Paige Billin-Frye. p. cm. –
(All aboard books) Summary: Text and illustrations provide
information about the sun, moon, and planets that make up our solar
system. 1. Astronomy–Juvenile literature. [1. Solar system.]
I. Billin-Frye, Paige, ill. II. Series QB64.W55
1993 520-dc20 92-24469 CIP AC

ISBN 978-0-448-40517-9   39 40 38

WHAT'S OUT THERE?

A Book About Space

By Lynn Wilson
Illustrated by Paige Billin-Frye

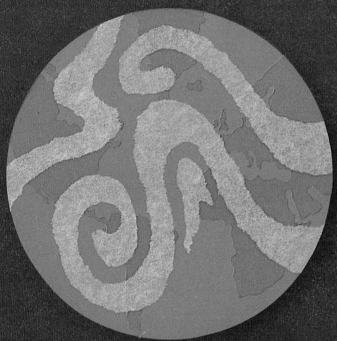

Grosset & Dunlap, Publishers

Out in the country, away from the bright lights of cities and towns, you can see that the night sky is filled with twinkling stars.

For thousands of years, people all over the world looked up at the stars and wondered what they were. They picked out groups of bright stars that looked like pictures of animals and people. The ancient Romans gave names to many of these star pictures—Leo the Lion, Taurus the Bull, Gemini the Twins, Orion the Mighty Hunter.

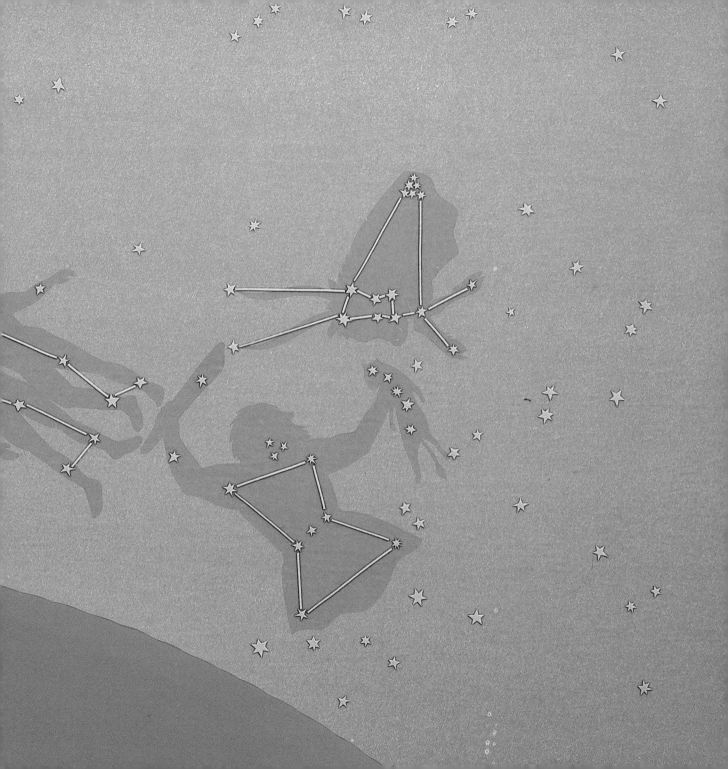

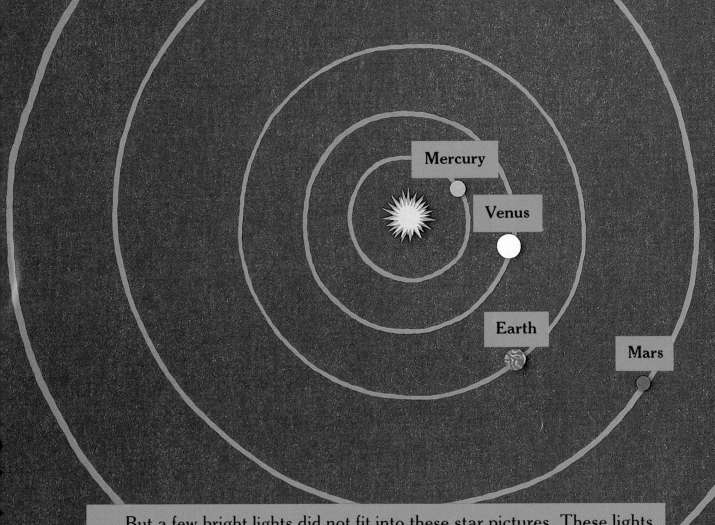

Mercury

Venus

Earth

Mars

But a few bright lights did not fit into these star pictures. These lights seemed to wander around in the sky. They were called planets, a name that means wanderers.

The Earth we live on is a planet. It is the third planet from the Sun. Can you find it?

The Earth travels around the Sun, along with seven other planets. Each planet follows its own path, called an orbit. Together, the eight planets and the Sun make up our solar system.

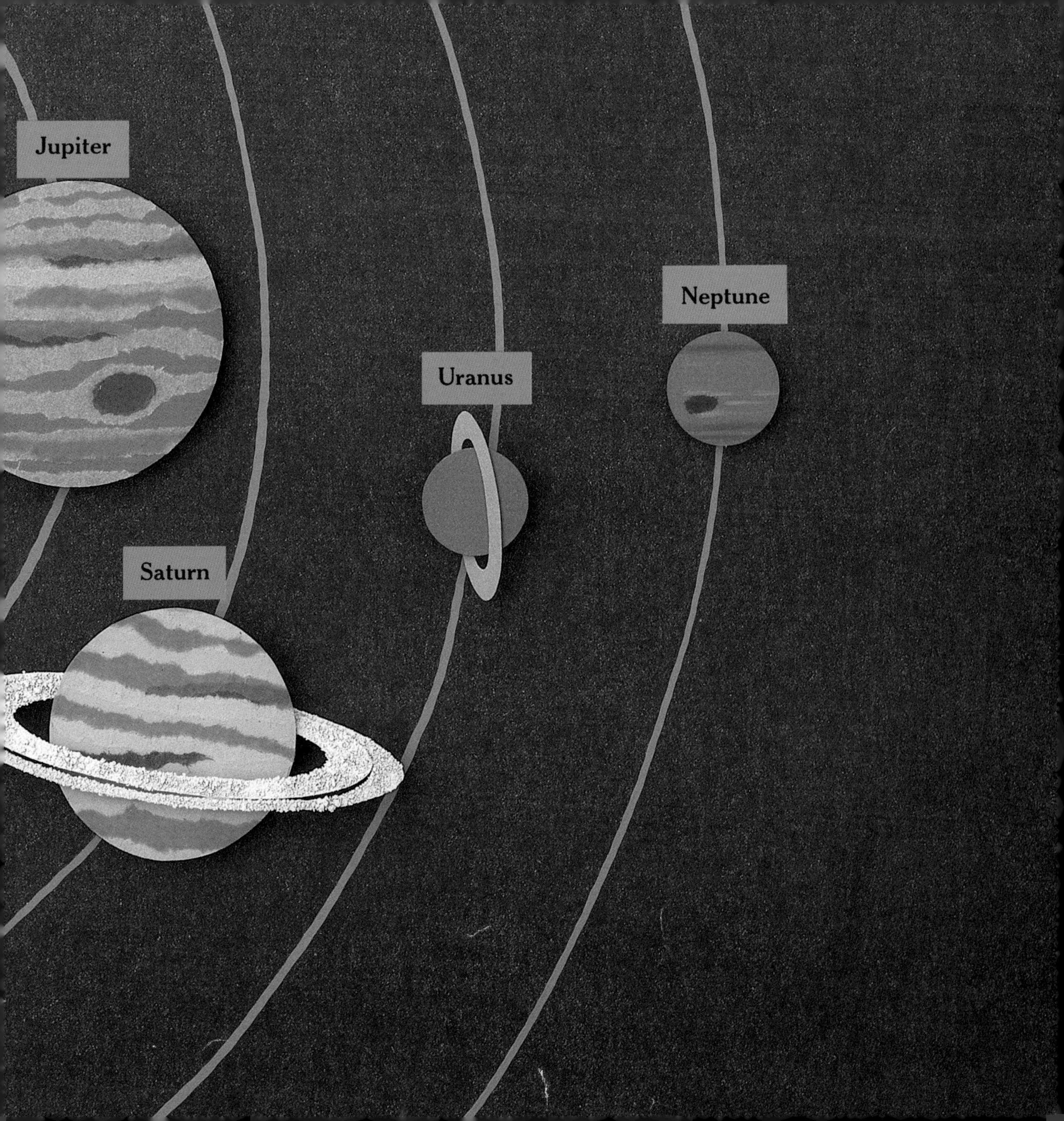
Jupiter
Saturn
Uranus
Neptune

The Sun is a star, just like the stars you see twinkling in the sky at night. It looks bigger and brighter than the other stars because it is so much closer to us—only 93 million miles away!

Like other stars, the Sun is a huge ball of fiery gases which give off heat and light. We need the Sun's heat and light for life on Earth.

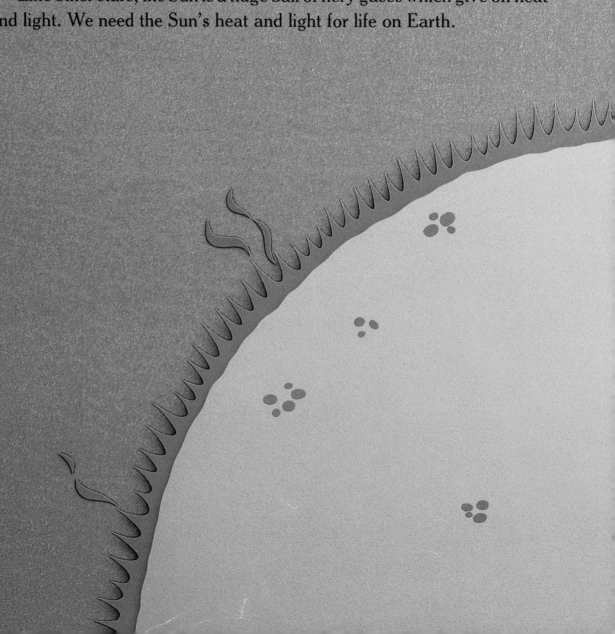

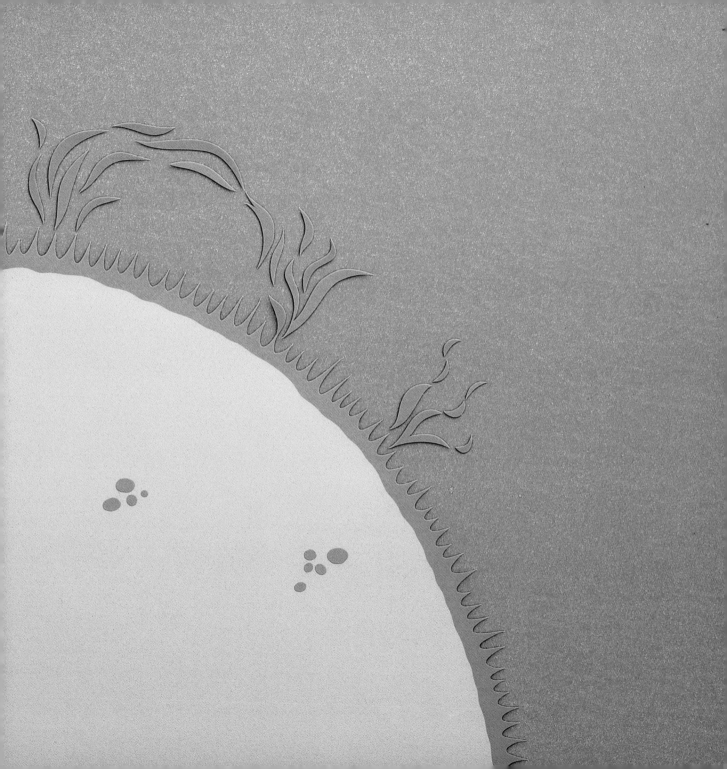

The planets do not give off any light of their own. All their light comes from the Sun's rays shining on them. The Earth's light comes from the Sun, too. The part of Earth facing toward the Sun has daytime. The part facing away from the Sun has nighttime.

Earth spins around and around—just like a top! So the part of Earth facing the Sun keeps changing. This is why day turns into night and night turns into day again. How long does it take for Earth to spin once around? It takes about 24 hours.

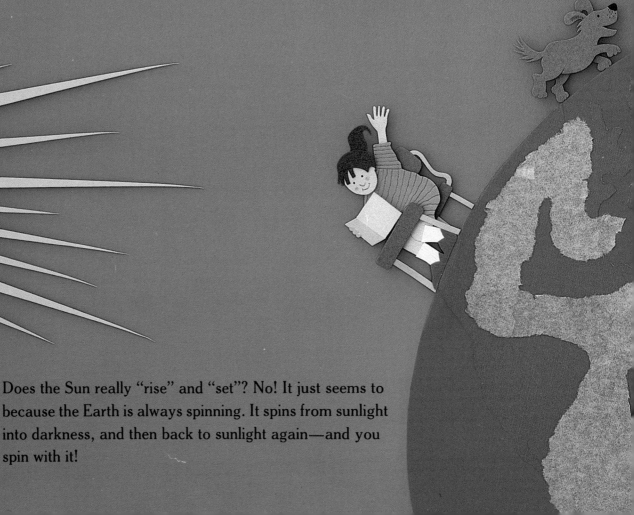

Does the Sun really "rise" and "set"? No! It just seems to because the Earth is always spinning. It spins from sunlight into darkness, and then back to sunlight again—and you spin with it!

Summer

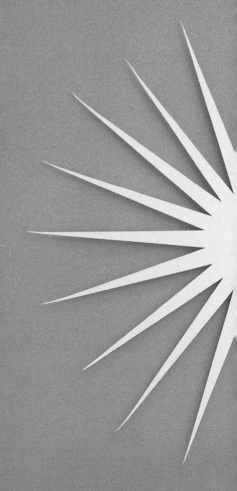

Besides spinning like a top, the Earth travels around the Sun. It takes about 365 days for Earth to go around once. This is why a year on Earth is 365 days long.

Because Earth is a little bit tilted as it travels around the Sun, our seasons change.

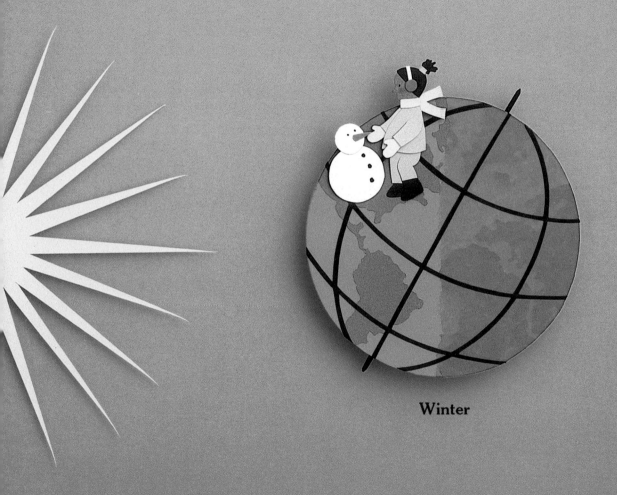

Winter

If the weather is warm and the days are long where you live, you know your part of the Earth is tilting toward the Sun. It is summer.

If the weather is cold and the days are short where you live, you know your part of the Earth is tilting away from the Sun. It is winter.

Crescent Moon

Half-Moon

Gibbous Moon

F

Just as the planets travel around the Sun, moons travel around the planets. Some planets have many moons. The Earth has just one.

Our Moon takes about 27 days—almost one month—to travel around the Earth. During that time, its shape seems to change.

Of course, the Moon doesn't really change shape. But as it moves around the Earth, sometimes the side facing toward us is lit up completely by the Sun. Sometimes it is lit up only part of the way. And sometimes it is not lit up at all!

on

Gibbous Moon

Half-Moon

Crescent Moon

As the Moon moves around the Earth,
we see only its lit up part.

The Moon is the only place in the solar system that people have traveled to from Earth.

The first person to walk on the Moon was an American astronaut named Neil Armstrong. He had fun walking on the Moon. He found that when he took a step, he bounced!

Why don't we bounce when we walk on Earth? Planets and moons have a force called gravity. The Earth's gravity is so strong that it pulls us down. It makes us heavy. The Moon's gravity is not as strong as the Earth's, so Neil Armstrong was not as heavy on the Moon. He was light enough to bounce. If you were on the Moon, you would be much lighter than you are on Earth, too!

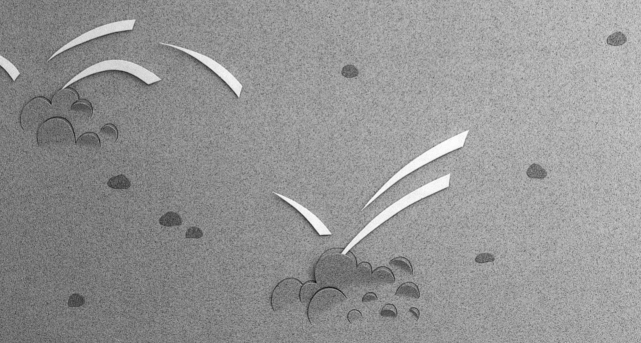

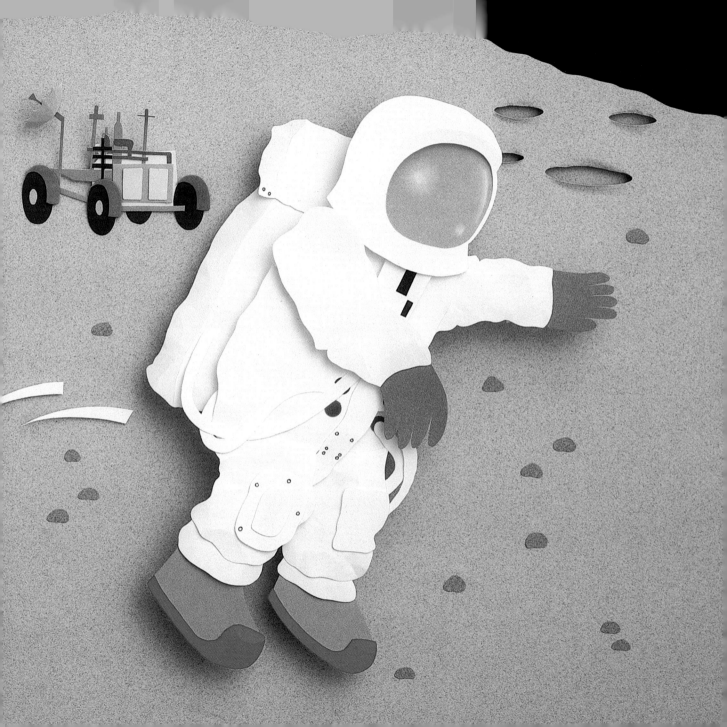

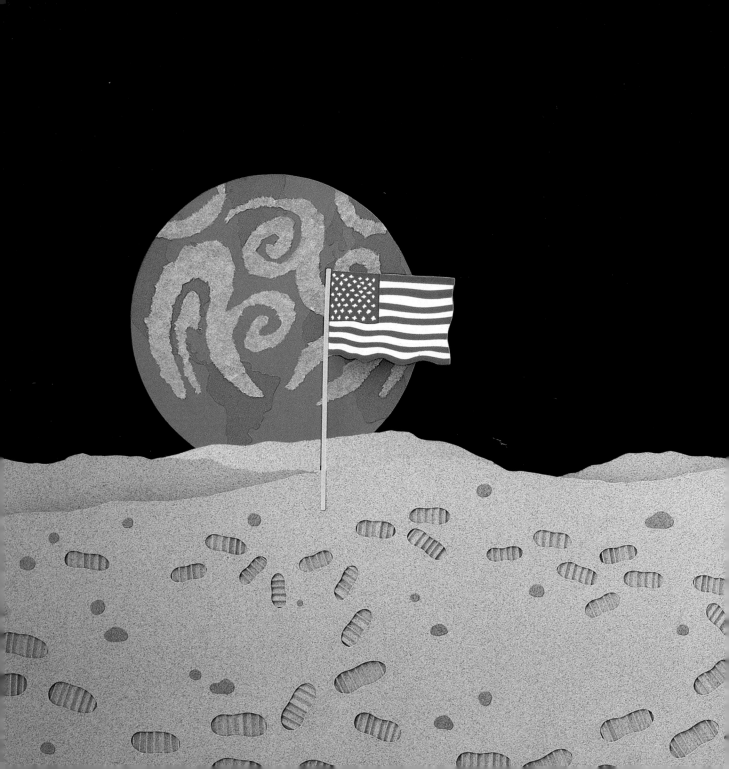

There is no air or water on the Moon. There are no plants or animals. Just rocks and dust. People have to wear space suits to stay alive.

On Earth, air and other gases catch the sunlight and spread it around. That is why our sky is blue. Since there is no air on the Moon, the sky is black all the time.

To a person standing on the Moon, the Earth is the biggest thing in the sky. It looks like a beautiful blue ball, covered with white clouds.

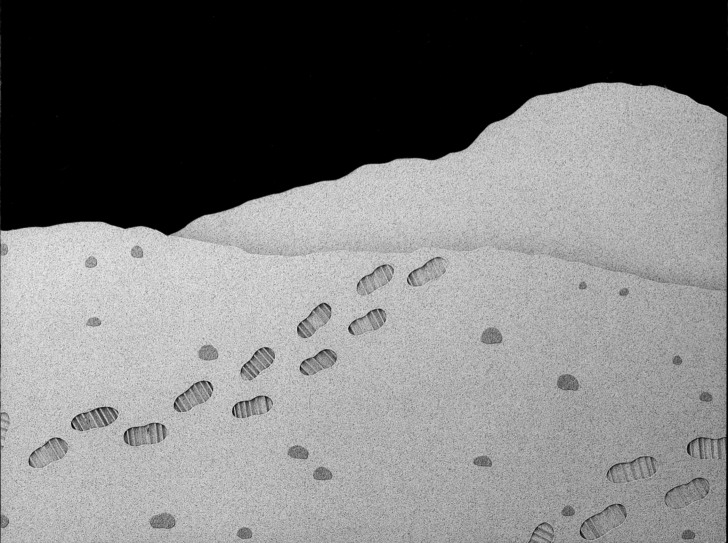

The Moon is our closest neighbor in the solar system. The planets Mars and Venus are our next closest neighbors.

For a long time, people thought these planets must be a lot like the Earth. Some scientists even thought they could see signs of life on Mars.

No human being has ever visited Mars, but during the 1970's, we sent rockets there. The rockets dropped robots down on the planet.

The robots took pictures of Mars. Their robot arms picked up samples of dirt and rock. They did not find any definite signs of life.

Mars has some ice, but no oceans or rivers. The air is not like our air, and people cannot breathe it.

Even so, Mars is more like the Earth than any other planet. Millions and millions of years ago, there may have been rivers on Mars. There may even have been life of some kind. No one knows for sure.

We know that the solar system is mainly empty space. Even the closest of the planets are more than 25 million miles away from Earth.

The first four planets in the solar system, called the inner planets, are alike in some ways. They are all made of rock and metal.

Mercury is the planet closest to the Sun. It takes just under three months to travel around the Sun. It has no air at all.

Venus comes next. It is very, very hot— almost 900°F—because clouds of poisonous gases hold in the Sun's rays.

Earth, the third planet, is the only planet with oceans. Gases surrounding Earth let in the good rays of the Sun, and keep out others that are bad for living things.

Mars, the fourth planet, is cold. Its air is thin and poisonous.

The next three planets are farther apart. These planets, called the outer planets, are huge—much, much bigger than the Earth. But they are not solid like the Earth. They are made of liquid and frozen gas. Under the gas, there is probably a solid center of rock and metal.

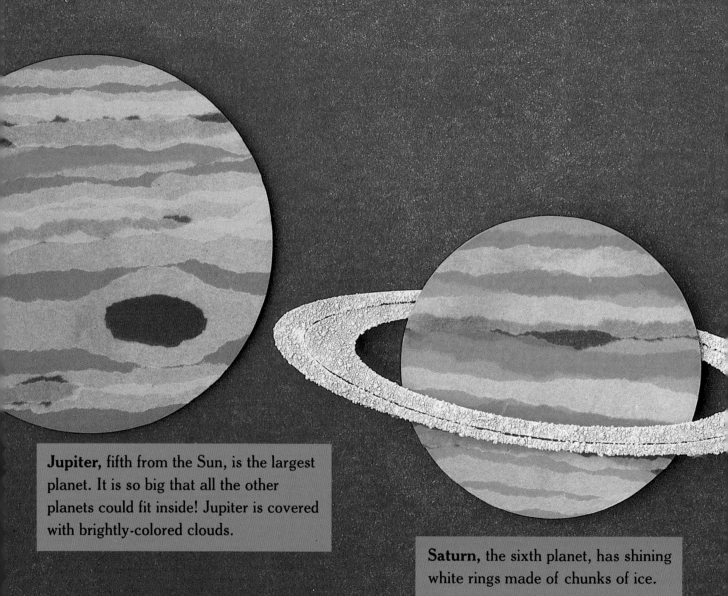

Jupiter, fifth from the Sun, is the largest planet. It is so big that all the other planets could fit inside! Jupiter is covered with brightly-colored clouds.

Saturn, the sixth planet, has shining white rings made of chunks of ice.

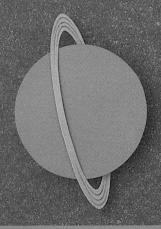

Uranus, the seventh planet, looks blue,
like the Earth. But its blue color is caused
by poisonous gases.

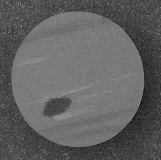

Neptune, the eighth planet, is very far
away and hard to see. In 1977, we sent
a spacecraft to take pictures of Neptune.
It took 12 years to get there!

Scientists used to believe that Pluto was
the ninth planet, but now they know it is
a dwarf planet.

Besides planets and their moons, the Sun and stars, what else is out there in the solar system?

Chunks of rock travel around the Sun, just as the planets do. They are called **asteroids.**

Other chunks of rock are called **meteoroids.** Most meteoroids are very small. When a meteoroid flies near the Earth, the force of gravity pulls on it. As it flies through the gases that surround Earth, it catches fire and burns up. Then it is called a **shooting star!**

Comets are out there, too. A comet is like a dirty snowball, whizzing through space. Comets are made of frozen gas, rocks, and dirt. When a comet gets near the Sun, the pieces of dust and ice that trail behind it begin to glow. It looks as if the comet has grown a tail!

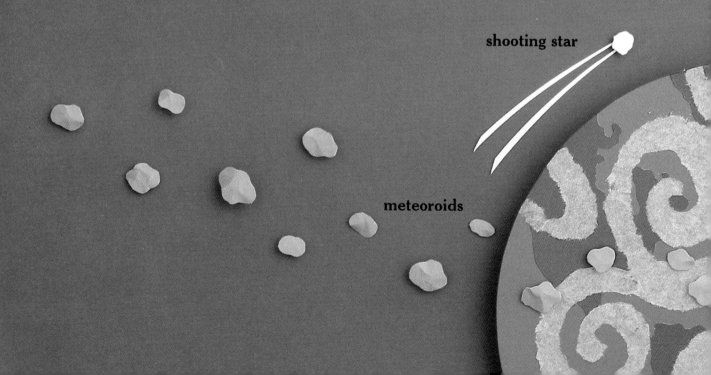

shooting star

meteoroids

comet

asteroids

The more we know about the universe, the more we realize how special our Earth really is. The Earth has plenty of water. It is not too hot or too cold. The air is good for living creatures. In the whole solar system, there is not another place exactly like it.

The Earth is our home in space!